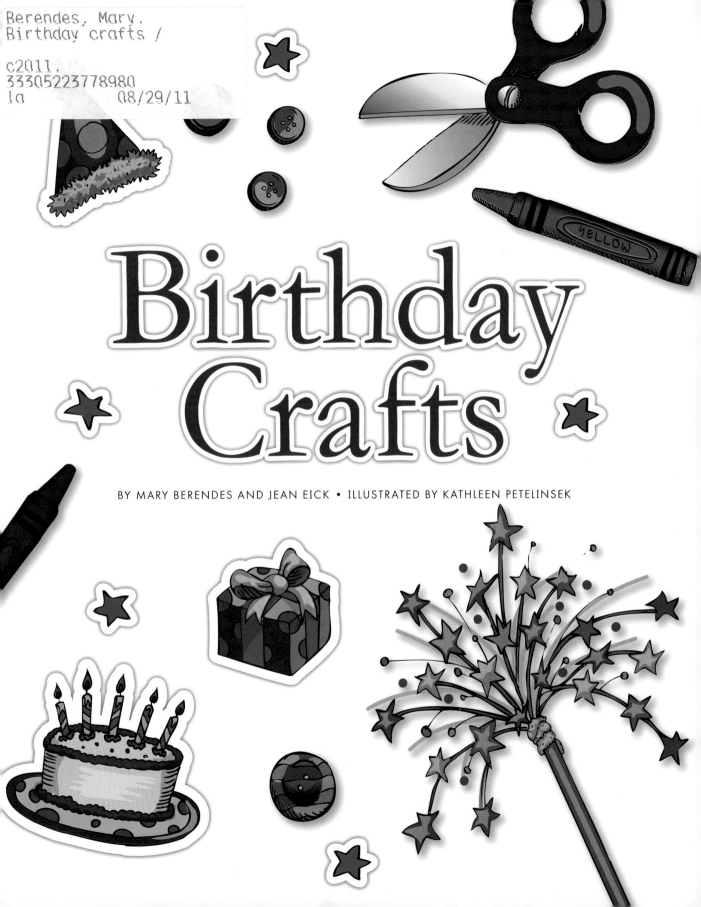

Birthday Crafts

BY MARY BERENDES AND JEAN EICK • ILLUSTRATED BY KATHLEEN PETELINSEK

The Child's World®

Published by The Child's World®
1980 Lookout Drive
Mankato, MN 56003-1705
800-599-READ
www.childsworld.com

The Child's World®: Mary Berendes, Publishing Director
The Design Lab: Design and production

Library of Congress Cataloging-in-Publication Data
Berendes, Mary.
  Birthday crafts / by Mary Berendes and Jean Eick;
illustrated by Kathleen Petelinsek.
    p. cm.
  ISBN 978-1-60954-231-3 (library bound: alk. paper)
  1. Handicraft—Juvenile literature. 2. Birthday parties—Juvenile literature.
I. Eick, Jean, 1947– II. Petelinsek, Kathleen, ill. III. Title.
  TT160.B46 2011
  745.594'1—dc22   2010035496

Printed in the United States of America
Mankato, MN
December, 2010
PA02071

Table of Contents

Happy Birthday!…4

Let's Begin!…6

CRAFTS

Birthday Sparklers…8

Birthday Yard Signs…10

Party Noisemakers…12

Pasta-box Frame…14

Pencil Holder…16

Birthday Cards…18

Envelopes…20

Activities…22

Glossary…23

Find More Crafts…23

Index…24

Happy Birthday!

Birthdays are very special days—everyone has a birthday! On a person's birthday, we **celebrate** the day that person was born.

People have celebrated birthdays for thousands of years. In many **cultures**, the birthday person is given presents. Some people have a party with friends and family. There is often a lot of food, music, and games. In some countries, having a special cake with candles is a great way to celebrate. No matter where you are in the world, a birthday is a happy time!

Let's Begin!

1 This book is full of fun and interesting ideas you can do to make a wonderful and special day for someone. There are ideas for decorations, gifts, and cards. There are activities at the end of this book, too!

2 Before you start making any craft, be sure to read the **directions**. Make sure you look at the pictures too—they will help you understand what to do. Go through the list of things you'll need and get everything together. When you're ready, find a good place to work. Now you can begin making your crafts!

Birthday Sparklers

These bright decorations are easy to make and fun to use at the party!

THINGS YOU'LL NEED

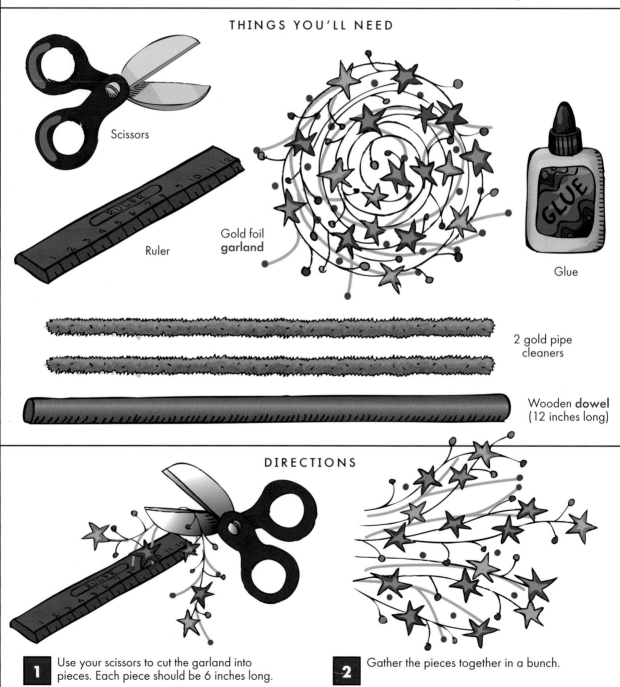

Scissors

Ruler

Gold foil **garland**

Glue

2 gold pipe cleaners

Wooden **dowel** (12 inches long)

DIRECTIONS

1 Use your scissors to cut the garland into pieces. Each piece should be 6 inches long.

2 Gather the pieces together in a bunch.

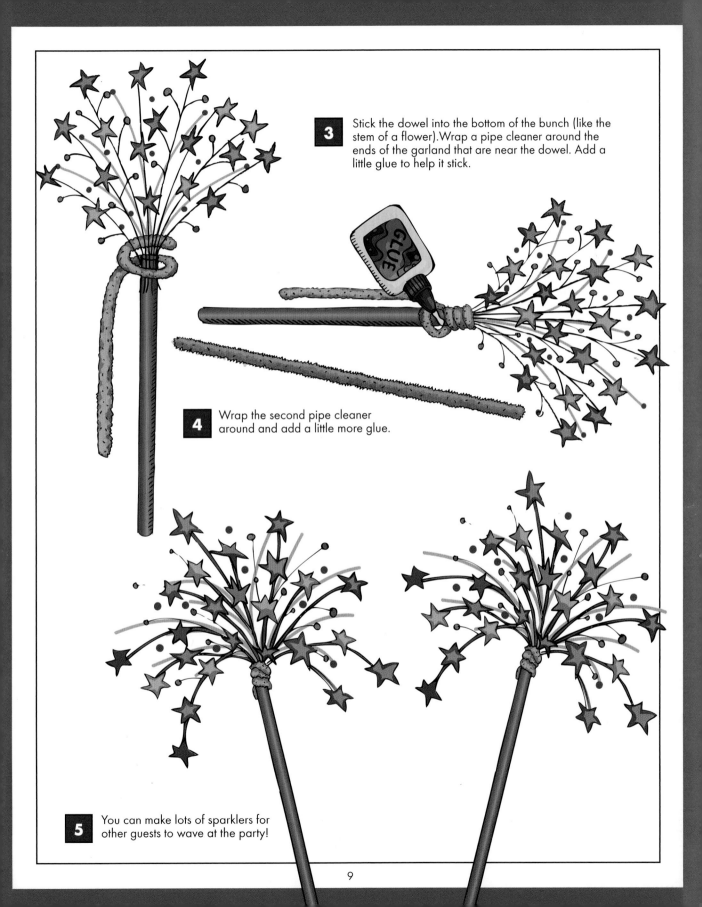

3 Stick the dowel into the bottom of the bunch (like the stem of a flower). Wrap a pipe cleaner around the ends of the garland that are near the dowel. Add a little glue to help it stick.

4 Wrap the second pipe cleaner around and add a little more glue.

5 You can make lots of sparklers for other guests to wave at the party!

Birthday Yard Signs

The birthday boy or girl will feel extra-special when they see these signs.

THINGS YOU'LL NEED

Scissors

Wrapping paper

Pictures and stickers for decorating

Pencil

Markers or crayons

Glue

Hole puncher

Ribbon

Lawn-care sticks (these come with little signs)

Poster board

1 Take the little signs off the sticks. Lay the signs on the poster board. Use your pencil to trace around the signs. Be sure to trace the hole, too!

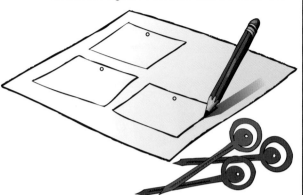

2 Cut out each sign.

3 Use the hole puncher to make a hole where you traced one.

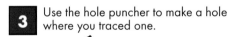
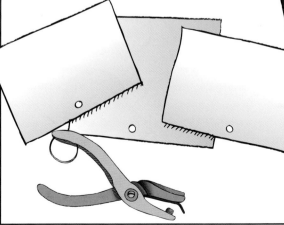

4 Decorate each sign any way you'd like. You can make silly pictures, bright animals, or even the numbers of the birthday the person is celebrating. Be sure to make one sign that reads "Happy Birthday!"

5 Put each sign onto the sticks. Push the sticks into the ground. Pick an area that can be easily seen, such as along the sidewalk or near the doorway.

Party Noisemakers

Celebrate a special birthday with lots of silly noises!

THINGS YOU'LL NEED

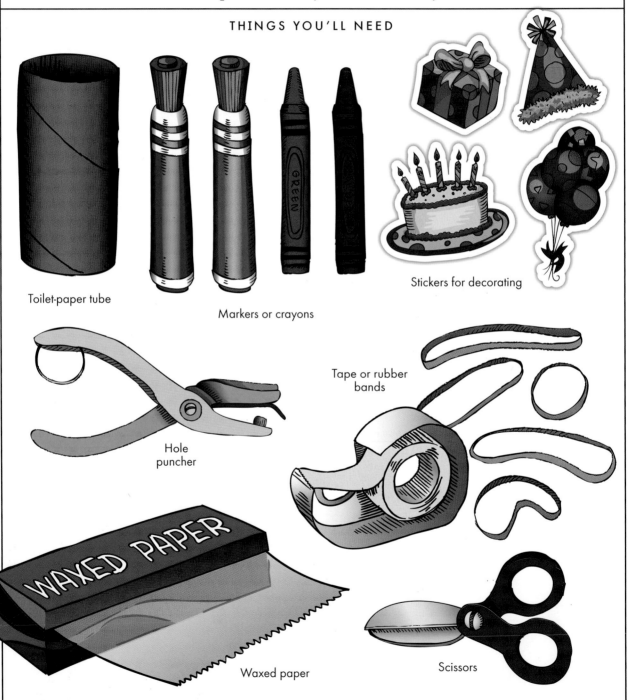

Toilet-paper tube

Markers or crayons

Stickers for decorating

Hole puncher

Tape or rubber bands

Waxed paper

Scissors

DIRECTIONS

1 Use the hole puncher to make a hole about 1 inch from an end of the toilet-paper tube.

2 Cut a piece of waxed paper so that it is about 4 inches by 4 inches.

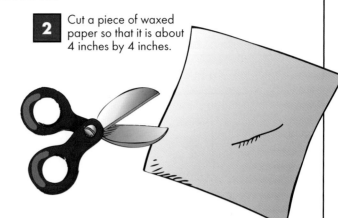

3 Place the piece of waxed paper over the end of the tube with the hole.

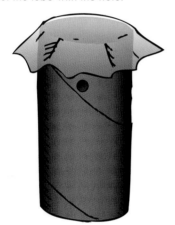

4 Tape the paper in place, or use rubber bands to hold it in place.

5 Decorate the tube any way you'd like.

6 Make silly noises and songs by humming into the open end of the tube!

Pasta-box Frame

This is a fun birthday gift for any friend, parent, or teacher.

THINGS YOU'LL NEED

A picture of you and the birthday person together

Construction paper

Magnet strip

A pasta box (the kind with the window)

Pencil

Glue

Buttons

Scissors

Glitter

Tape

Markers or crayons

Stickers

DIRECTIONS

1 Cut around the window of the pasta box. You can make wavy edges, straight edges, or any shapes you want.

2 Use your pencil to trace this shape on the back of the pasta box. Cut out the shape (this will be the back of your frame).

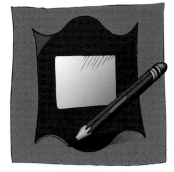

3 Take the picture and center it in the window. Tape it in place. Trim any extra edges that stick out.

4 Glue the back of the frame to the front.

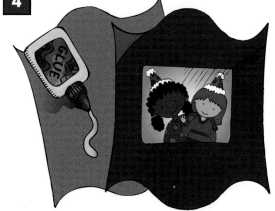

5 Decorate the frame with your markers, crayons, wrapping paper, and stickers.

6 When all the decorations and glue have dried, glue the magnet strip to the back of the frame. Now your friend can hang your gift on their refrigerator!

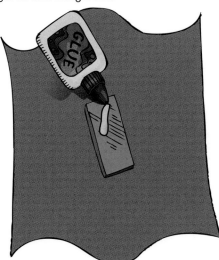

Pencil Holder

This makes a great gift for holding pencils, crayons, or other things.

THINGS YOU'LL NEED

Scissors

Construction paper

A clean soup or juice can

Pencils or other items to fill your pencil holder

Wrapping paper

Glue

Ribbon

Buttons

Glitter

Stickers

1 Glue the construction paper or wrapping paper all the way around the can

2 Decorate the can any way you'd like. You can cover it with stickers, glitter, or even cool buttons. Tie a ribbon around the can if you'd like.

3 Fill the can with pencils and crayons to make a nice birthday gift.

Birthday Cards

Giving cards is a very popular idea. You can send them to friends, teachers, and other special people.

THINGS YOU'LL NEED

Scissors

Construction paper (lots of different colors)

Glue

Buttons

Ribbon

Pencil

Markers or crayons

Glitter

Stickers

DIRECTIONS FOR CARD ONE

1 Fold a piece of construction paper to the size you want it to be. Folding once will make a large card. Folding it twice will make a smaller card.

2 Decorate the front of the card any way you'd like. You can use ribbons, buttons, glitter, and stickers. You can even use magazine pictures that remind you of parties or of the person who's having the birthday. Good ideas are balloons, **confetti**, and cake. Write a message on the inside of the card. You can decorate the inside, too. Don't forget to sign your name!

DIRECTIONS FOR OTHER CARDS

1 You can make birthday cards in many different ways. Here are some ideas for making your cards even more special! Place your hand on the front of the card and use your pencil to trace around it. Then decorate your handprint with crayons, markers, or glitter.

2 For a flower card, glue colored strips and a cotton ball to the front of the card. They should make a flower shape.

3 For a picture card, find a nice photograph of you and the person celebrating their birthday. Glue the picture to the front of the card and decorate all around it.

Envelopes

You can make your own envelopes to fit your homemade cards.

THINGS YOU'LL NEED

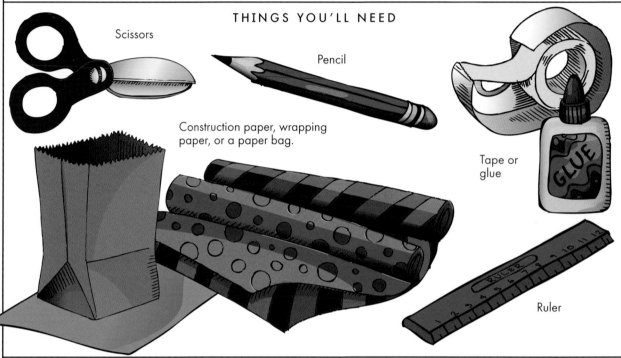

Scissors

Pencil

Construction paper, wrapping paper, or a paper bag.

Tape or glue

GLUE

Ruler

DIRECTIONS TO MAKE A SQUARE ENVELOPE

1 Cut out the front of a plain paper bag.

2 Use your ruler and pencil to mark a square that is 8 inches long on each side. This will be big enough for a 5 ¼-inch card. Mark an "x" in the center of your square (4 inches in from each side).

3 Fold three of the corners so they cover the "x." Tape or glue the corners so they'll stay in place.

4 Place your card inside. Fold the top down and tape it shut.

DIRECTIONS TO MAKE AN ENVELOPE THAT'S NOT SQUARE

1 Use your ruler and pencil to mark a square on a large piece of construction paper or wrapping paper. The paper must be 4 inches taller and 5 inches wider than your card. Draw a line 2 inches down from the top.

2 Fold the top down along the line.

3 Place your card under this flap.

4 Fold in each side over your card.

5 Fold up the bottom.

6 Now take your card out of the envelope.

7 Glue the sides of your envelope together. Don't glue the top, however! You have to be able to put your card back inside!

8 Fold up the bottom and glue it in place.

9 Put your card back inside. Fold down the top flap and tape the envelope shut.

Activities

Birthday parties are fun times to do things with your friends.
Here are some fun things to do together.

1 ## Balloon Catch

Have everyone at the party stand in a big circle. The birthday boy or girl is "It" and stands in the middle of the circle. Have everyone count off. The person who's "It" then throws a balloon up high and calls a number. The person with that number must catch the balloon before it touches the ground—or they're "It" for the next round!

2 ## Dog Catcher

Have everyone at the party stand in a big circle. The birthday boy or girl is "It" and stands in the middle of the circle—blindfolded. Have everyone walk around the circle slowly. The person who's "It" grabs someone from the circle. The grabbed person says "Bark! Bark!" in a silly voice. If the "It" person can't guess who's barking, the game goes on. If they guess correctly, the "barker" is now "It."

Glossary

celebrate (SELL-uh-brayt) When people celebrate something, they do something happy and fun. Having a party is a great way to celebrate a birthday.

confetti (kon-FET-tee) Confetti is tiny pieces of paper that are thrown in the air during celebrations.

cultures (KUL-churz) Cultures are people's ways of life and traditions. In many cultures, people give gifts on a person's birthday.

directions (dir-EK-shunz) Directions are the steps for how to do something. You should follow the directions in this book to make your crafts.

dowel (DOW-ull) A dowel is a rounded stick. Dowels can help you make fun crafts.

garland (GAR-lund) A garland is a spiral of something, such as flowers or leaves. A star garland makes a great birthday sparkler.

Find More Crafts

BOOKS

Bull, Jane. *The Best Craft Book Ever.* New York: DK Publishing, 2006.

Druitt, Ann, Christine Fynes-Clinton, and Marije Rowling. *The Birthday Book: Celebrations for Everyone.* Gloucester, England: Hawthorn Press, 2004.

WEB SITES

Visit our Web site for links to more crafts: childsworld.com/links

Note to Parents, Teachers, and Librarians: We routinely verify our Web links to make sure they are safe and active sites. So encourage your readers to check them out!

Index

activities, 22

balloon catch, 22

cake, 5

cards, 18

celebrating, 4, 5

dog catcher (game), 22

envelopes, 20

history, 5

noisemakers, 12

parties, 5, 22

pasta-box frame, 14

pencil holder, 16

sparklers, 8

yard signs, 10

ABOUT THE AUTHORS

Mary Berendes has authored dozens of books for children, including nature titles as well as books about countries and holidays. She loves to collect antique books and has some that are almost 200 years old. Mary lives in Minnesota.

Jean Eick has written over 200 books for children over the past forty years. She has written biographies, craft books, and many titles on nature and science. Jean lives in Lake Tahoe with her husband and enjoys hiking in the mountains, reading, and doing volunteer work.